About the Author

LUKE PEMBERTON works in the political department of a large international organisation dealing with the prevention of international conflict and post-conflict crisis management. This is his first book.

LUKE PEMBERTON

HOW to FIND your WAY OUT WHEN IN DESPAIR

SilverWood

Second Edition published by SilverWood Books

SilverWood Books Ltd
14 Small Street, Bristol, BS1 1DE, United Kingdom
www.silverwoodbooks.co.uk

ISBN 978-1-78132-772-2 (paperback)
ISBN 978-1-78132-779-1 (ebook)

British Library Cataloguing in Publication Data
A CIP catalogue record for this book is available from
the British Library

Page design and typesetting by SilverWood Books
Printed on responsibly sourced paper

To my wife Heike and sister Anna

Contents

Introduction

This book is not intended to be an academic account of the various forms of mental health issues and psychological problems that people may face throughout their lives. It is also not intended to cover in detail each form of trauma and or abuse that may affect people at various stages of their lives. What it is intended to be, however, is a very candid personal account of my experience in dealing with unfortunate negative childhood experiences which had a detrimental effect on my emotional and psychological development for many years.

In describing my experience, I hope that others may recognise similar issues in their lives and seek the help they need. This book is therefore aimed at such people. I hope it will also be useful for friends and family of someone who is experiencing emotional and psychological pain who may wish to educate themselves in a small way in order to be able to help the person concerned.

The account is based on my experience of having had poor mental health for pretty much my whole life. My particular problem was that I suffered from chronic anxiety on an almost permanent basis. I assumed it was just the way I was made and I struggled through life until I just couldn't go on anymore. This was partly because I had no real idea what proper mental health felt like. I subsequently realised that my chronic anxiety was linked to a form of emotional abuse I experienced as a child.

'Anxiety' and 'emotional abuse' are loaded terms, of course, so let's look at them a bit more closely.

The NSPCC (National Society for the Prevention of Cruelty to Children) defines emotional abuse as the ongoing emotional maltreatment or emotional neglect of a child.

While the emotional abuse I suffered was of a passive nature, I am confident that this book will also be very relevant to those who suffered other forms of abuse.

Turning back to my experience of passive emotional abuse, this consisted of the following (selectively taken from the NSPCC's website):

- Developmentally inappropriate interaction with the child, e.g. expecting the child to perform tasks that they are not emotionally mature enough to do.
- Failure to recognise a child's individuality; this can mean an adult relying on a child to fulfil their emotional needs and not recognising that the child has needs.
- Emotional unavailability: where a parent or carer is not connected with the child and cannot give them the love that they deserve and need, never showing any emotions in interactions with a child, also known as emotional neglect.
- Negative attitudes, such as having a low opinion of the child and not offering any praise or encouragement.

Passive emotional abuse can be just as damaging as other forms of child abuse. Physical or sexual abuse is often easier to pinpoint and victims may be able to recall specific, concrete incidences. Passive emotional abuse is more insidious. This is because it happens subtly over long periods of time, slowly tormenting the child until he develops psychological problems, often without his ever realising that anything is amiss.

Regarding the broader symptoms, Mind, the British mental health charity, defines anxiety as follows (www.mind.org.uk/media/619080/understanding-mental-health-problems-2014.pdf):

Anxiety can mean constant and unrealistic worry about any aspect of daily life. If you are feeling anxious, you may feel restless, experience sleeping problems and possibly physical symptoms; for example, an increased heartbeat, an upset stomach, muscle tension or feeling shaky. If you are highly anxious, you may also develop related problems, such as panic attacks, a phobia or obsessive-compulsive disorder (OCD).

(Please also see Mind's excellent booklet *Understanding Anxiety and Panic Attacks* for more information on this particular topic: www.mind.org.uk/media/1892482/mind_anxiety_panic_web.pdf.)

I also subsequently suffered from depression, which primarily stemmed, in my case, from the psychological pressure I was under for many years, a topic which I address briefly later in the book. (Mind also has an excellent booklet on this topic: www.mind.org.uk/media/42904/understanding_depression_2012.pdf.)

Regarding the book's structure, the first part focuses on the cause of my problems, followed by an account of how these manifested later in my life, as I approached middle age. The second section explains how I dealt with and gradually resolved these issues, with the help of a psychotherapist and subsequently a psychiatrist.

Since the terms used to describe mental health specialists, e.g. psychologist, psychotherapist, psychiatrist and counsellor, may be confusing and easily misunderstood, they are explained here. In my case I saw a psychotherapist who helped me look at how my past experiences had affected my emotional development and my adult life through 'talking therapy'. I subsequently also saw a psychiatrist, somebody with significant medical training who can prescribe medication to counter illnesses such as depression. More information on talking therapies is available on the NHS website. Please note that I include a number of online resources in Section 3, Managing the Therapy Process – Some Practical Tips, including on how to find help and the various forms of help available.

I decided to include illustrations throughout the book because I know how exhausting suffering from poor mental health can be and I wanted to keep things as simple and as 'digestible' as possible.

Although the suicide rate in general has steadily fallen over the last 30 years or so (for both sexes, although more for women in comparison with men), the figures remain upsetting. The excellent Campaign Against Living Miserably (www.thecalmzone.net) notes that:

> In 2014 there were 6,109 suicides in the UK, of which 76%, or 4,623, were male, and suicide currently stands as the biggest single killer of men aged under 45 in this country. The ratio of male to female suicide has shown a sustained rise over the last 30 years. In 1981 men accounted for 62% of suicides in this country, which rose to 70% in 1988, 75% in 1995 and hit 78% in 2013.

A recent article in *Esquire* magazine stated that men in the UK aged 20 to 49 are now more likely to die from suicide than any other cause of death, and that the figures are chilling, and yet still it is something we hardly discuss, in public or private – which is a significant part of the problem itself.

Looking more closely at the statistics, I was shocked to find that many of these men seemed so similar to me, i.e. normal blokes with families, jobs, normal interests, similar ages etc. Alas, for these poor men, it is too late for sympathy. However, I very much hope that this short, simple recollection of my experiences will be able to at least help others in a small way.

Finally, I would like to add that this book is not intended as a diatribe against my parents; quite the reverse. My parents are both very good, warm and intelligent people who were trying to parent as best they could under often trying circumstances, in the face of various social factors and based on their own experiences as children. Also, there has been a dramatic increase in society's understanding of child development needs and psychological issues in general, which has occurred in the space of just one generation, an understanding that was not available to my parents' generation.

Part 1

Understanding Things Before Finding the Way Out

I'm probably very similar to you.

This is me. 45 years old happily married, great job and kids.

Beer belly forming.

But I had a secret.

I would put my happy face on every day but deep down I was in despair.

I almost always felt the following:

They all seem so comfortable and confident in themselves.

Life felt a bit like this to me:

Me crawling. Other people running without drawing breath.

I often felt crushed by a sense of real inadequacy.

I was sleeping badly very often and felt exhausted all the time. I would regularly have bad dreams and I felt permanently anxious and emotionally vulnerable and insecure. How come everyone else seems refreshed, fairly confident and relaxed?

What is it that I just don't get? What is wrong with me?

I would often have disturbing thoughts.

Some of these thoughts were of an X-rated, adult nature and were very disturbing and upsetting.

Sometimes these were of a sadomasochistic nature.

In addition I would often have repetitive dreams about being abandoned.

"I'm going to Australia for three months on my own, bye!" (My beautiful wife.)

In short, I was very sad, confused, exhausted and in despair.

My general approach to problems at the time was fairly logical, e.g. if I felt physically unwell, I would go and see a doctor, take any medication required, rest and take it easy. If I wanted to invest my money better, I would go and see an expert, read up on the subject and ask friends for advice. However, my approach to my most pressing and fundamental problem, namely my sense of total despair, was very illogical.

I feel in total despair. I know, I won't see a doctor and I don't want to read about my issues. I'll just go to the pub more often and get really smashed.

One day I suddenly had the urge to jump out of a high window.

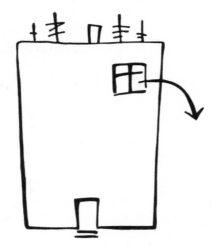

Note: although this book is written purely from a layman's personal experience, it goes without saying that if you've had similar thoughts to the one above you should seek help immediately.

"SOS, HELP!"

I realised I had to do something. Acknowledging this was a big step.

So I went online… Google.

'Campaign Against Living Miserably'

This led me to psychotherapy.

Going through the door the first time meant me swallowing my pride.

Actually doing it is one of the most important steps in the right direction.

After a few sessions with my psychotherapist...
I realised I had deep emotional insecurities.

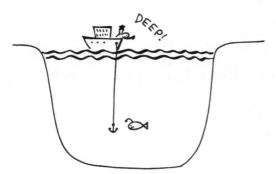

A. It's Got a Lot To Do With Your Parents (Well, Probably)

I realised quickly that it all had a lot to do with my parents.

My Relationship With My Mother

After discussion and a fair amount of reflection I started to realise that, deep down, my relationship with my mother was not as I had always thought.

I always felt I was a burden to my mother and that I was making her sad.

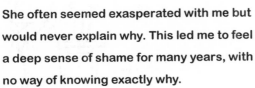

She often seemed exasperated with me but would never explain why. This led me to feel a deep sense of shame for many years, with no way of knowing exactly why.

This caused me to feel intense shame. Shame is very different from guilt. Guilt is 'I have done something bad', whereas shame is 'I am bad'. Shame is the key emotion, and we'll look at this closely a little later.

In addition…

My mother often felt and expressed stress and despair.

Kids are almost telepathic in their ability to sense and feel the emotions of their parents.

I felt her emotions keenly and often. This added to my sense of insecurity, as I was concerned and confused by her behaviour and my possible role in causing it.

My mother also used me for emotional support when I was very young. This was very confusing to say the least. This is known as maternal enmeshment.

"You are such a burden to me but you are also my saviour! I can unload all my distress and worries onto you, because you will never leave me."

"You are so much more important to me that your father. I want you to be my surrogate husband."

"Um, ok…very confusing sexually, but of course I'll do it. I'm a man now!"

I feel like I now exist within her and I have no room inside me for my own emotional development. I feel totally intertwined with her emotions. It's a really uncomfortable, suffocating and humiliating feeling. Let me out!

It felt like this all the time: my mother and myself emotionally bound together. After a while:

"I'm still not happy – you haven't done enough for me. Anyway, I prefer your younger brother now so I'll just ignore you. Bye…"

Wow, I've just been 'dumped' by my own mother. I feel humiliated, emasculated and totally betrayed.

This sense of betrayal at an early age stuck with me, and had rather comical effects later in life.

Local man selling his *Big Issue* homeless magazine and thanking a lady for being his most favoured customer.

Me overhearing this and becoming insanely jealous at being 'betrayed' by this local man, as I thought I was his favoured customer.

Additionally, my emotional barriers were never really developed and were trampled upon by my mother, meaning I became very vulnerable and unable to properly protect myself emotionally.

Me and my healthy emotional barrier.
My personal emotional space.

Looking back…

I wish I could have put my Boba Fett costume on and defended myself against this 'alien' invasion. I could also have used my lightsaber which would definitely have done the trick.

My Relationship With My Father

In therapy I also discussed my relationship with my father. My experience with my mother meant I was somewhat more vulnerable to feeling rejected by my father. It didn't help that, as a child, my relationship with him was characterised by the following types of exchange:

"Please go away, I'm busy"

or

"Sorry, but I don't have time for you at present"

or

"I'm reading my newspaper."

I'm obviously not worthy of his attention. There must be something wrong with me but I'm too stupid to work out what it is, although everybody else is aware of it. I feel humiliated.

Or

My father always seemed to have more time for other people. I feel really small and insignificant.

I 'idealised' my father. This allowed me to subconsciously convince myself that his apparent lack of interest in me was because he was so important and busy. It also allowed me to feel important myself purely by association with him.

I kept trying to get my father's attention like a submissive poodle. It was 'death by a thousand cuts'.

I always felt like I could not connect with him. This turned out to be 'crazy-making'.

It reached a point where I would create fantasy stories...

My primary school teacher.

Me making up stories about what a great weekend I had just had with my father, and what amazing things we had done together (a bit tragic, really...).

But she knew I was making these stories up because she was a good friend of my parents...

Then I thought that I had worked it out.

I've worked it out! If I can prove myself to my father, then he'll be proud of me and acknowledge me.

I know, one day I will win
the British Open Golf
Championship.

Me winning. My father, full of
pride running towards me.

Or perhaps he'll notice me
and love me if I become Prime
Minister.

My father, full of pride running
towards me.

My mother added to the unreality and inaccuracy of my image of my father
– this rather alien person who would on occasion suddenly appear in my life –
by sometimes using his image to threaten my siblings and me.

"If you are not a good boy your father will be very angry."
Gulp, I'm scared.

As a result, I created a very distorted and threatening image of my father in my mind. He looked a bit like this to me:

I'm really scared of this person.

Apparently I would often scream and refuse to be in the same car as him when I was very young.

On reflection...

I also wished I had used my lightsaber to zap and destroy the newspapers that my father always seemed to be reading (but in reality I had broken it two hours after opening it in an epic battle with my brother and his lightsaber).

The Theatre Analogy (and More on Theatres and Plays Later)

This image of being on stage in front of my extended family and others often came to my mind.

When I take centre stage I see myself as this repulsive, distorted, hideous creature.

This is a very Kafkaesque image for me.

They are all expecting me to perform my 'life script' to perfection.

Me on stage, consumed by 'toxic shame'.

Members of the seated audience, primarily family members, parents, aunts, uncles, ect. My father is so disgusted by what he sees that he faints and has to be carried out of the theatre by aunts and uncles who berate me for doing this to him.

This is because a child's view is naturally 'ego-centric' i.e. if anything seems to go 'wrong' in a child's narrow world, the child often views him/herself as being at fault.

What I Thought my Mother was Conveying to Me, and How I Interpreted It

- You have upset me but I won't tell you why – *I am a burden; my mere presence is problematic; I am bad.*
- You have to make me happy – *This is a huge responsibility; she thinks I am a man; I must not upset her; I must neglect myself for her benefit, otherwise I will be abandoned.*
- I am still not happy – *I have failed my own mother during her hour of need; my ability to take on and solve other people's burdens determines my right to exist and whether I will be accepted or not.*
- I'm now going to spoil your brother and will ignore you – *The 'contract' we had whereby she gave me everything in return for my love is now annulled. I'm being punished for my inability to make her happy; I feel fundamentally betrayed, humiliated and emasculated; I must avoid this ever happening again as it feels awful.*
- It upsets me when you put your friends before me – *I must always put my mother first; I should be ashamed of attending to my own needs.*
- I am submissive to your father – *I should also be submissive to him, and by default to other people. This is how relationships work best.*

What I Thought my Father was Conveying to Me, and How I Interpreted It

- Sorry, I'm busy at the moment – *I don't deserve his attention.*
- I choose to ignore you in public – *I'm ashamed to recognise you as my son. I won't protect you in any way; you will always be vulnerable.*
- I can't talk to you now; I have to call somebody on the telephone – *I am a burden; other people are much more important than I will ever be; he is right to ignore me.*
- I treat other people with more respect and attention than you – *I will never command respect and I will always be a little boy, never becoming a man.*
- Silence – *I am too stupid to even work out why he doesn't want to talk to me; I must be defective as a person; I feel very anxious in his presence; I must prove myself to him, then he will accept me.*

The Overall, False Conclusions I Drew from My Interaction With My Parents

- I am not worthy of my parents' attention; I am therefore not worthy of anybody's attention. There is obviously something very wrong with me, and I am too stupid to realise what it is (although everybody else has been able to work it out).
- The problem must be in my make-up, as my siblings seem more confident and respected.
- This feeling of victimisation is awfully confusing; why is it that I make all the effort to give people what they want and yet I am the one who is punished for not being enough for people, and for not being enough for God as well?
- I must prevent this from ever happening again. I must redouble my efforts at pleasing people, being submissive, and doing exactly what they want, otherwise I will be abandoned and alone all my life.
- As a result, I should be ultra-critical of myself and punish myself for the

slightest misdemeanour; otherwise I will just never learn. I am clearly not worthy of being loved. I must therefore create an 'internal Torquemada' to scrutinise my every move and thought.

- If something bad happens, or if anybody regards me as not being good enough, then it will always be my fault and I should apologise accordingly. If something good happens, then it is as a result of somebody else's efforts, not mine.

Parents' Self-Esteem and the Child's Self-Esteem

For further information on the vital role parents play in determining the self-esteem of a child, take a look at a very interesting report by the Joseph Rowntree Foundation published in 2001, entitled *Self-esteem: The costs and causes of low self-worth*, and an associated BBC article.

Same Parents, Different Childhood

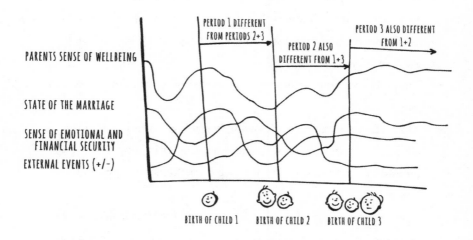

HOW THREE SIBLINGS CAN HAVE QUITE DIFFERENT EARLY EXPERIENCES IN LIFE DEPENDING ON THE DYNAMIC NATURE AND HEALTH OF THE FAMILY SYSTEM

It is amazing how siblings growing up together in the same family unit can experience quite different childhoods, depending on the changing family dynamics, social situation etc.

B. Overcoming Other Negative Experiences in Childhood

Many of us may have undergone other damaging emotional experiences growing up (such as being bullied at school). For me, one set of such experiences was undergoing religious education (or indoctrination, as one could define it). Although my experiences with my parents made me more susceptible to the negative aspects of religious teaching (or indoctrination), it had a profound effect on me.

The Big Man in the Sky Can Read Your Mind – Religion and Childhood Fears

Nuns at my Junior School. Remember, above all you are a lowly sinner and you should always say sorry to God for failing him.

Gulp, so now Mum, Dad and God are not happy with me but I still don't know why.

The notion from Christianity that we are all 'born sick but commanded to be well' sat easily with me.

I am destined to remain childlike all my life.

In God's eyes, you are like a baby sheep, and he is your shepherd. He is your all powerful, eternal Father. You will always be a child to him.

Remember, I'm doing this for you.

And never forget this.

Gulp, gosh. I'm so sorry that it was partly my fault that he was tortured and executed…

But don't worry. All you have to do is to prove to Jesus all the time that you are good enough to be allowed to go to heaven and not be abandoned for all of eternity. And remember, he knows and sees everything.

I really identified with Jesus Christ, somebody who it is said sacrificed himself for the benefit, or 'saving' of others, thinking, "If I am submissive and sacrifice all my needs for those of other then people will be eternally grateful to me and then I wont be forgotten".

Bad Joke Interlude

I realise the content of this book can sometimes be a little 'heavy' so here is a rubbish joke to lighten the load a bit.

A man walks into a zoo.

The only animal there was a dog.

It was a shih tzu.

Childhood Fear is Existential Fear

I felt too inhibited to confront my parents with my anger and frustration so all my energy was redirected back at myself in the form of self-hatred.

My childhood fears of my parents were existential fears that I might die without them.

I'm a burden to them both. I must be perfect otherwise they will be right to leave me and then I could die.

37

These existential fears were buried in my 'basement' and continued until I uncovered and faced them in therapy.

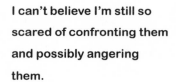

I can't believe I'm still so scared of confronting them and possibly angering them.

You need a lot of courage to overcome these deeply embedded existential fears from childhood.

Should I even be allowed to exist? All these childhood experiences leave you feeling like a faint shadow of a person, with no real sense of self, no emotional barriers to protect yourself, very confused emotions and a deep sense of insecurity about yourself.

And they made me very scared. A child's fear is very different from an adult's fear. An adult can put things into some form of perspective. For a child, any hint that the parents might not be there for him or her strikes right at the heart of the child's existential fear of death.

Existential fear of abandonment!

My mother. She is fed up with me.

My father. He appears disappointed in me.

I felt like a permanent child when I was growing up (and did so until therapy in fact), in a land full of giant grown-ups whose world I could never enter, a 'policy' they had decided for me when I was an infant. If I continued my 'script' of being a polite, inoffensive boy, then maybe they would let me in for brief moments.

39

The Opposite of Rose-Tinted Glasses – Life Through Distorted Lenses

All these experience create a very distorted prism through which I saw the world.

I have to prove myself to every new person I meet.

If I am submissive and apologetic, then women will approve of me and like me.

Confirmation Bias – Belief À La Carte

Confirmation bias is a tendency to only look for information that confirms one's (often false) preconceptions. Everyone is susceptible to this, but especially children.

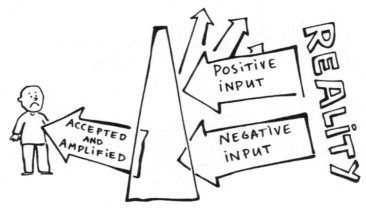

My lens, prism, filter (distorted).

Positive messages/input rejected.

Any real or neutral input with possible negative connotations accepted and amplified.

This is called confirmation bias.

"See, I know I am bad and that the world is hostile."

C. The Effect of These Experiences on my Sense of Self

The heart of the matter

My greatest fear was that I was not good enough to be loved.

My Internal Torquemada – the Ability to Punish Oneself Mercilessly

It's amazing how self-critical you can become. You end up treating yourself like the most awful person that has ever lived. You develop a side of yourself which is similar to Tomás de Torquemada, the first Grand Inquisitor in the Spanish Inquisition.

My Torquemada part of me: as soon as I had a hint of positive thought, this part of me would immediately crush it and attack me with total ruthlessness. This became so debilitating and frustrating. Part of me became so intent on hating and punishing myself I nicknamed it Torquemada from the Spanish

Inquisition. I was in total conflict with myself, so I had to learn to understand why and to begin to love myself fully, battling the power of my Torquemada along the way.

'Heretic punishment awaits!'

Fed and supported by all the built-up anger from childhood that I could not express at the time.

My 'House of Character' Built on Quicksand

To put it simply, my childhood experiences had created a very weak foundation on which to build my 'house of character'.

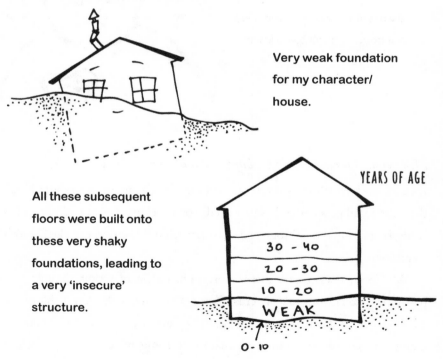

Very weak foundation for my character/ house.

All these subsequent floors were built onto these very shaky foundations, leading to a very 'insecure' structure.

42

I always had the feeling my parents were on my shoulders. There voices of disapproval never seemed to leave me. It was very draining and frustrating.

"You still don't understand why I'm withholding my love for you, do you?"

"Why don't you get it?"

"What's wrong with you? Everybody else knows…"

"Why aren't you making more of an effort?"

"Don't disappoint me! Work and try harder!"

In addition, I honestly believed that God was ever-present in my mind and was scrutinising every single thought I had for signs of 'thought crimes' (weird, I know, but that's religious indoctrination for you).

A 'heaven transmitter' in my mind allowing God to scrutinise every single thought I was having.

For forty years I believed that God was scrutinising all my thoughts, putting a lot of pressure on myself to not be convicted of a thought crime. Weird, I know…

This sense of being punished, rejected and shamed, as well as victimised, felt like being on death row. I never knew when the next possibly (existentially) fatal blow might come from, and from whom.

(This is partly why I identified so much with Franz Kafka's novel *The Trial*, heartily recommended if you have ever felt the same way.)

I wish somebody had told me the following:

- Challenge all your assumptions.
- It was not your fault.
- It did not happen the way you think it did.
- Your mother and father love you very much.
- Everything is going to be just fine.

D. Shame – the Elephant in the Room

I feel a very heavy weight on my shoulders, a key emotion that I just can't put my finger on yet...

The emotion that overwhelmed me when I was growing up, and which is key to all of this, is shame. If you can understand the damage that this does, and may have done to you too, then you are halfway to resolving your issues. Shame has often been regarded as the secret epidemic.

The Difference Between Guilt and Shame

Guilt vs. Shame

I am bad.

I did something bad.

Many people suffer from it, often as a result of childhood experiences, but because of its nature too few people talk about it or are even properly aware of it.

Shame in childhood need not be destructive; however, too much over the tipping point can be almost irreversible.

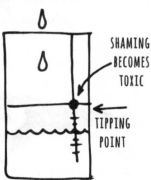

SHAMING BECOMES TOXIC

TIPPING POINT

45

Too Much Shame as a Child Can Become Toxic

Toxic shame eats away at you from the inside out until you are completely hollowed out of any positive emotion. It feels like a cancer of the soul.

It then completely fills you with up with a feeling of total self-contempt, up to your eyeballs, so that you feel swamped with its effects from the inside out.

You become shamed to the core of your being and it overpowers all other emotions you have. It appears at the forefront of your mind every waking moment and poisons every emotional reaction you have with the world.

The more it overwhelms you, the greater the self-contempt becomes and the less willing you are to ever help yourself. It then thrives in the world of silence that you create around it.

It totally shrinks you as a person in a vicious circle of self-recrimination until you are an emotional black hole.

This black hole within you looks to suck in any negative messages it can come across. You become masochistic and look for ways to hurt yourself emotionally. This toxic shame 'parasite' takes you over and feeds on this self-contempt.

Just like Obelix, Asterisks's companion and the magic potion cauldron.
It feels like I was dropped into a cauldron of toxic shame as a child and it stayed toxic within me forever.

I therefore often felt that these fears and emotions would engulf me.

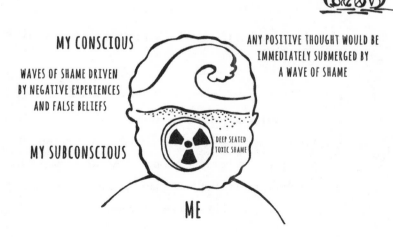

MY CONSCIOUS

WAVES OF SHAME DRIVEN BY NEGATIVE EXPERIENCES AND FALSE BELIEFS

MY SUBCONSCIOUS

ANY POSITIVE THOUGHT WOULD BE IMMEDIATELY SUBMERGED BY A WAVE OF SHAME

DEEP SEATED TOXIC SHAME

ME

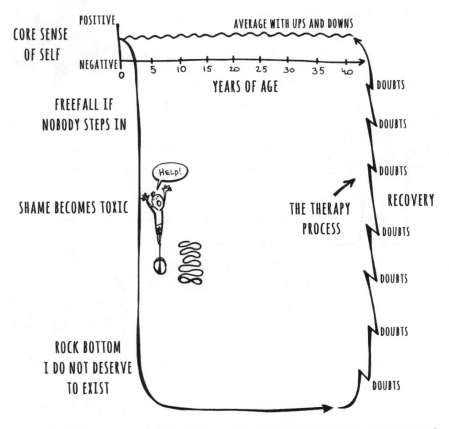

MY SELF-HATRED IS COMPLETE (NOT ENOUGH SPACE TO SHOW HOW DEEP THE DESCENT IS)

An Insect Named Franz – the Analogies of Franz Kafka

I really associated with Franz Kafka in his novel *Metamorphosis* when he turned into a horrible human-sized insect in his bedroom. To my mind Franz Kafka was clearly a victim of toxic shame at a young age, leading him to see himself in such repulsive ways.

E. Carrying All This 'Emotional Baggage' into Later Life

I must be very careful how I behave and what I say.

I felt too insecure to ever assert myself or confront my parents, or even to show any anger or frustration.

These unaddressed fears came with me into my adult life. This led me to feeling very exposed and vulnerable and fearful, as I knew I didn't have the ability to defend myself as a result of these deep childhood fears.

Every time I met a new person before therapy I had a feeling of foreboding. I would think to myself, "Another new person that I have to prove my worth to before they will accept me – more work!"

At the time, I treated all my friends almost like business clients, i.e. like people I had to continually impress and prove my worth to otherwise I feared they would take their friendship elsewhere.

I also put all my friends on huge pedestals. I was, as a result, never willing to disagree with or question them in any way. I therefore came across as very submissive and pliant. This led to lots of complications in my mind, e.g. I would be subconsciously resentful if they overlooked me for something – "After treating them so well I expect some form of payback, please" – a ridiculous way to approach a relationship.

As soon as I got into a debate with anyone, I immediately thought, "Ok, they've got me on this one. They are clearly going to win this debate," no matter how ridiculous their comments.

My first girlfriend was one of these friends.

"Oh my gosh, she is so beautiful (and she was). I cannot believe she is interested in me. She is going to see the real, hideous, grotesque, repulsive and repellant me, and then she is going to dump me and run a mile. I am really scared…"

At the time my subconscious was telling me, "My own mother 'dumped' me. If I was not good enough for her, what chance do I have with this lovely, stunning beauty?"

Slow train crash. And then the inevitable happened, because I was so stupendously insecure around her. I was totally devastated and my confirmation bias kicked in big time, to the point where I felt sorry for her for having the experience of being with me.

(Me to myself) "See, I knew I was not worth anything."

"I'm really sorry, but this just isn't working."

Subconsciously, I was imagining her telling all our close friends, and them all deriding her for even considering going out with me in the first place (and all these friends are in reality the nicest, most caring, most magnanimous people you could ever meet).

In fact… For years I had images of even my best friends wanting to mock and belittle me. It was only when I found the source of my sense of shame that these very upsetting images stopped.

Just keeping my head above water, i.e. just surviving, was exhausting.

My negative thoughts threatened to drag me down under water.

My whole life felt like I was continually 'spinning plates' to keep my life from collapsing.

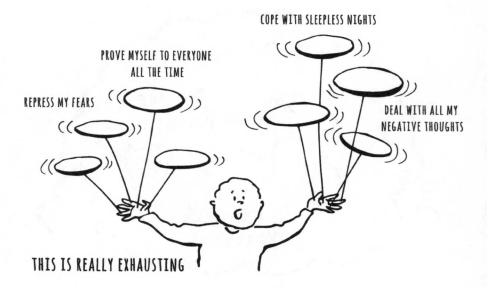

All these pounding waves made me feel
emotionally overwhelmed, confused,
disorientated and mentally 'breathless'.

Sailing the Seven Seas — a Maritime Analogy of My State of Mind

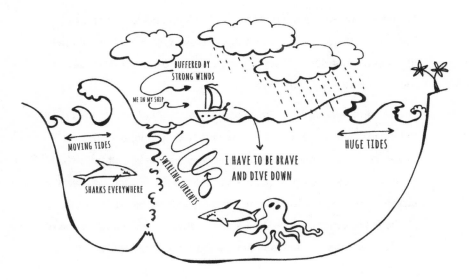

Another rubbish joke to keep you going...

What's the worst thing about being a vegan?

Getting up at 05:00am to milk the almonds.

F. The Emotional Black Hole – Burnout and Depression
Too Much Emotional Baggage – How Psychological Pressure Can Crush You

I must always prove my right to exist to everybody I meet. The
Torquemada part of me wants to destroy myself. My true place in
life is in the shadows. I must always please God, or no heaven for
me. I am ashamed of my body.

I must succeed hugely in life to gain my father's acceptance. I hold
myself in contempt and it's right for me to be punished. I have so
much frustration, anger, confusion and pain that I don't have the
right to express. I will never be a man, just a perpetual child with an
insignificant voice. I feel so unbelievably vulnerable all the time.
I believe I have less worth than a paedophile. I can find no sense of
self-love or respect in myself at all and this is very frightening.

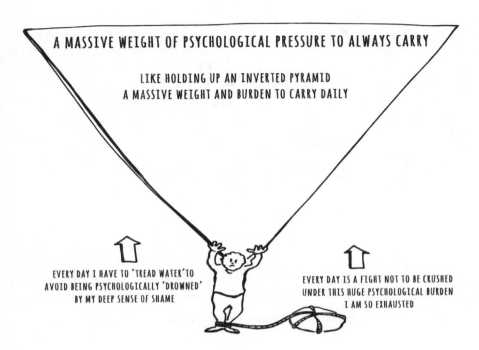

A MASSIVE WEIGHT OF PSYCHOLOGICAL PRESSURE TO ALWAYS CARRY

LIKE HOLDING UP AN INVERTED PYRAMID
A MASSIVE WEIGHT AND BURDEN TO CARRY DAILY

EVERY DAY I HAVE TO 'TREAD WATER' TO
AVOID BEING PSYCHOLOGICALLY 'DROWNED'
BY MY DEEP SENSE OF SHAME

EVERY DAY IS A FIGHT NOT TO BE CRUSHED
UNDER THIS HUGE PSYCHOLOGICAL BURDEN
I AM SO EXHAUSTED

I have no sense of my own psychological needs. My mother's happiness always comes before mine (and, by extension, everyone else's). If I can't even 'attract' my mother, then I am ugly to all females. I am very scared of my parents. I deserve no rest.

Bringing all my difficult subconscious feelings etc into an already crowded mind proved too much for me.

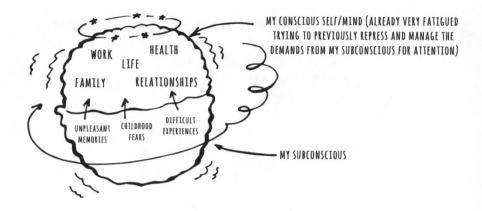

MY CONSCIOUS SELF/MIND (ALREADY VERY FATIGUED TRYING TO PREVIOUSLY REPRESS AND MANAGE THE DEMANDS FROM MY SUBCONSCIOUS FOR ATTENTION)

WORK
HEALTH
LIFE
FAMILY
RELATIONSHIPS

UNPLEASANT MEMORIES
CHILDHOOD FEARS
DIFFICULT EXPERIENCES

MY SUBCONSCIOUS

I found myself thinking about emotionally difficult issues more and more. Warning signs were not obeyed and I fell into a negative cycle of over-analysing issues. The more I tried to 'think my way out', the worse it became.

My brain on a treadmill. Treadmill at full speed relentlessly. Just as a runner's legs give up eventually, so did my mind.

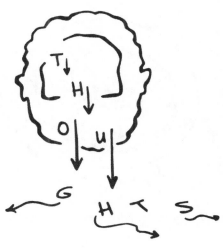

Suddenly it felt as if all the thoughts in my mind just fell apart and fell out of my mind. I had had a nervous breakdown.

I was burnt out...

and fell into depression.

I felt like my mind had collapsed in on itself like a collapsing star and become like a black hole into which all my energy had been sucked.

I used to lie motionless on my bed for hours.

Even making toast became an extreme effort and thinking positively about the future was a challenge too far.

Luckily my boss was very understanding, as was my doctor.

The only real way to recover from depression and burnout is rest and good sleep, proper medication from a psychiatrist and lots of healthy food and exercise.

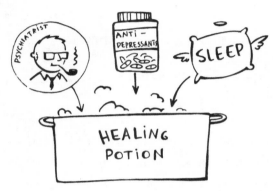

Seeing a Psychiatrist

Anti-depressants + sleeping medication.

Rest and lots of much-needed sleep.

Alcohol – a Good Servant but a Terrible Master

What you shouldn't do, of course, is the most tempting thing of all, at least for me, which was to go boozing in the pub.

Alcohol alleviated my suffering for short periods of time (although I needed more and more each time), but increased the severity of my depression.

Momentary pleasure from alcohol (declining effect), followed by a worsening of the depression.

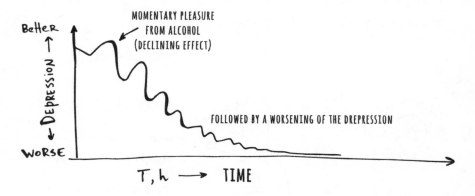

These episodes proved too much for me. They also resulted in a very unpleasant feeling of mental exhaustion that weighed on me all the time. Alcohol provided my only respite from feeling this way. At first it was a pleasant experience and limited to a few beers. Then after a while I started to live for the evenings when I could go out and get really smashed. Suddenly I ended up in an alcohol treatment centre for four weeks to enable me to recover from what had essentially become an addiction. It's amazing how alcohol creeps up on you, as depression does, and has you in its clutches before you know it.

Alcohol for me was like a wolf in sheep's clothing. It 'bit' me quite a few times before I realised this.

DR JEKYLL	MR HYDE	PARTNER/FRIEND
DORMANT YET STRONG	DORMANT FEARS AND	CONFUSED, HURT,
FEELINGS OF FRUSTRATION,	FEELINGS FLOOD OUT	ANGRY
FATIGUE, ISOLATION,	WHEN DRUNK	
DEPRESSION AND FEAR		

G. Dealing With Troublesome Thoughts

Before we move on to finding the way out, I tried not to be afraid of the troublesome thoughts that often occurred to me as I was going through a sustained period of psychological pressure and tension. I let these thoughts come to me, pictured them clearly, and let them occur, rather than trying to repress or ignore them. Your therapist will be able to provide expertise on this matter.

I would often have troubling and uncomfortable thoughts about issues such as violence, homosexuality, and submissiveness.

I pondered, rationalised, and worked through these thoughts and images until they were resolved and stopped occurring (linked to my sense of toxic shame and associated frustration).

Additional Bad Joke Interlude

Really rubbish joke:

I started growing fungi recently. I'm using two small pots...

So I don't have mushroom to work with (bad, I know).

Part 2

Finding the Way Out

A. The Therapy Process and the Need to 'Re-Parent' Yourself

I undertook psychotherapy, or 'talking therapy', which is based on a patient's unconscious thoughts and interpretations that developed during childhood.

You talk about anything you want to (dreams, fears, football etc).

The therapist listens intently.

More information on this type of therapy is available here and here. Information on other forms of therapy is available from www.counselling-directory.org.uk/counselling.html.

If you are having problems pinpointing exactly what caused your emotional pain, then you may have to analyse things a bit more than others to find the cause(s). I took a bit of a Sherlock Holmes approach.

The real causes of passive, incremental emotional abuse are often frustratingly hard to pinpoint.

Sherlock Holmes investigates 'what exactly traumatised me'.

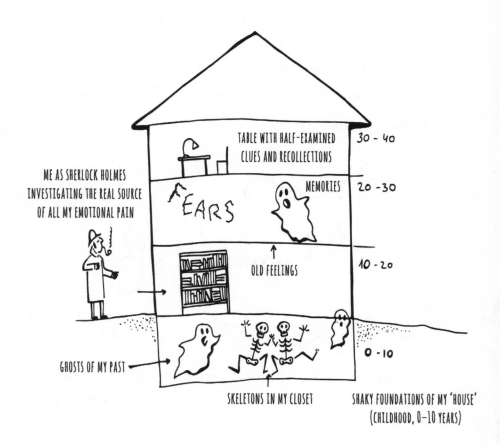

TABLE WITH HALF-EXAMINED CLUES AND RECOLLECTIONS — 30 - 40

MEMORIES — 20 - 30

ME AS SHERLOCK HOLMES INVESTIGATING THE REAL SOURCE OF ALL MY EMOTIONAL PAIN

FEARS

OLD FEELINGS — 10 - 20

GHOSTS OF MY PAST

0 - 10

SKELETONS IN MY CLOSET

SHAKY FOUNDATIONS OF MY 'HOUSE' (CHILDHOOD, 0–10 YEARS)

Chipping Away at the Granite Block of Issues in Your Mind

When I started doing therapy it felt
like there was a huge granite block in
my mind that was standing in the way
of my progress. It was a very strange
feeling.

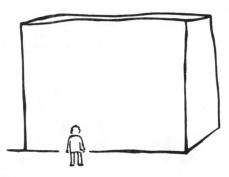

**This granite block now feels
about this big.**

**It took a lot of effort but it was
so worth it.**

The therapy process is a bit like Lord of
the Rings

Me slaying and conquering my deep-seated fears.

**Throwing my ring of toxic shame that had overcome me with its
power into Mount Doom.**

Inside the cellar I found the ghosts of my childhood relationships with my parents, which I just had to face.

These ghosts and other fears/gas leaks often came to the upper floors during my life and haunted me.

The idea of my therapy was to drill down through all these floors, then dig up the foundations and rebuild from the bottom up.

Anything else would have been like repainting the rooms without fixing the structural problems.

Some of the Issues and Emotions to be Discussed in Therapy May Include

Approval, consent, confirmation, independence, personal authority, affirmation, jurisdiction over oneself, autonomy, belief, belonging, legitimacy, hope, endorsement, self-respect, a voice, assent, self-compassion, love for self, courage to overcome existential fear, permissible, affirmation, acceptance.

Illegitimacy, burnout, vulnerability, exposure, sexual perversion, paranoia, self-disgust, shame, pain, depression, desperation, fear, confusion, isolation, abandonment, victimisation, distress, pressure, stress, insomnia.

Dreams – Wow, They Really Mean Something?

I discussed many of my recurrent dreams with my psychotherapist.

I had countless dreams of my wife simply leaving me for no apparent reason. I also had recurrent dreams of my first girlfriend not noticing or seeing me in social situations.

Me always trying to play golf in a very restricted space with no room to swing the club. Very limiting and frustrating.

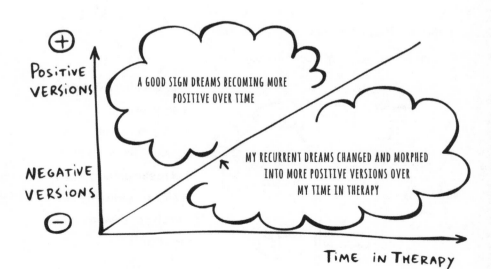

B. How to Free Ourselves by Understanding Our Life Scripts

Understanding how we interact with other people is a very useful way to understand why we act in certain ways. This approach to therapy was developed by Eric Berne and is called transactional analysis.

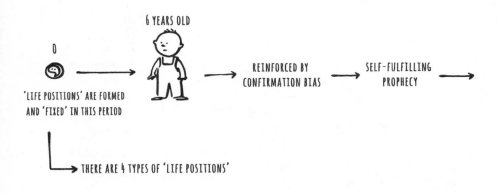

6 YEARS OLD

0

'LIFE POSITIONS' ARE FORMED
AND 'FIXED' IN THIS PERIOD

REINFORCED BY
CONFIRMATION BIAS

SELF-FULFILLING
PROPHECY

THERE ARE 4 TYPES OF 'LIFE POSITIONS'

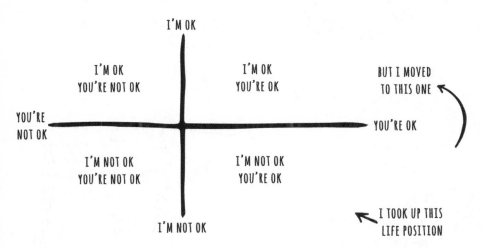

I'M OK

I'M OK
YOU'RE NOT OK

I'M OK
YOU'RE OK

BUT I MOVED
TO THIS ONE

YOU'RE
NOT OK

YOU'RE OK

I'M NOT OK
YOU'RE NOT OK

I'M NOT OK
YOU'RE OK

I'M NOT OK

I TOOK UP THIS
LIFE POSITION

The adopted 'life position' then determines the 'script' you follow for life, unless corrected.

Me following my adopted script, so that I can play my assumed 'role' in the theatre of life, just like in a play.

This was produced by me when I was a scared and under-developed small child. It was my best attempt in the circumstances but, with proper hindsight, can now be discarded.

Part of my script included:

"I'm allowed to exist as long as I try very hard all the time."

Whenever I tried to relax or be kind to myself, this part of my script would remind me of this role I had to play, making relaxation difficult.

Giving up this script is a bit like giving up and old teddy bear, i.e. something familiar, something that gave you comfort and a (false) sense of security.

The good news is that once you are aware of your role and script defined or adopted in childhood, then you can change or discard them, although this takes some effort as they are embedded.

So in this sense, Shakespeare was correct when he wrote, in *As You Like It*, that 'all the world's a stage; and all the men and women merry players'.

As a result of this script I would often fall back into a child-ego state and behave as if I was a little boy again.

There are three different ego states in this transactional analysis theory:

Child-ego state: Re-experiencing behaviours, thoughts and feelings left over from my childhood (often unresolved negative ones).

Parent-ego state: Copying behaviour from parents/ parental figures, i.e. behaving like your parents without really realising it.

Adult-ego state: Behaving as an independent and autonomous person.

The aim is to enable you to exist in a proper adult-ego state, meaning that one is an independent and autonomous individual.

Do you ever notice yourself falling into a child-ego state? I often fell into one, especially when I saw, for example, cousins or old friends I had not seen since my childhood and who only knew me as a child. Once you recognise this happening you can consciously snap out of it. It takes a bit of effort but it's a liberating feeling.

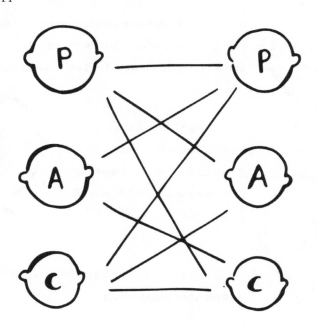

Falling into a child-ego state.

This is a good way to try and understand the interaction process between people. A process which depends on which of these three ego states each person happens to be in at the time.

C. The Importance of Connecting Emotionally With Yourself

Connect with yourself.

During this process...

I often felt like the character Jason Bourne in *The Bourne Identity*.

I need to find out who I really am and move away from this version of me formed so much by negative experiences at a very formative age (a bit different as he was brainwashed as an adult, but you get the idea).

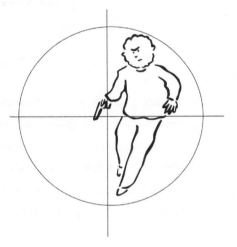

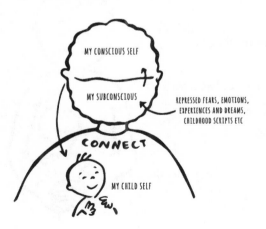

MY CONSCIOUS SELF

MY SUBCONSCIOUS

REPRESSED FEARS, EMOTIONS, EXPERIENCES AND DREAMS, CHILDHOOD SCRIPTS ETC

CONNECT

MY CHILD SELF

Repressing all my subconscious material is almost as much work as letting it all out and processing it properly.

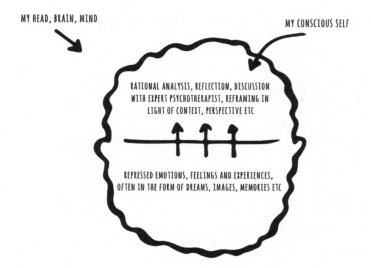

MY HEAD, BRAIN, MIND

MY CONSCIOUS SELF

RATIONAL ANALYSIS, REFLECTION, DISCUSSION
WITH EXPERT PSYCHOTHERAPIST, REFRAMING IN
LIGHT OF CONTEXT, PERSPECTIVE ETC

REPRESSED EMOTIONS, FEELINGS AND EXPERIENCES,
OFTEN IN THE FORM OF DREAMS, IMAGES, MEMORIES ETC

Through therapy you bring all the repressed emotions, feelings and memories from your subconscious back to your conscious self, where you can re-assess, re-interpret, understand and reframe these in a proper and rational manner. It's a bit like recalling data from a computer hard drive into its memory, where it can be used and processed.

I found it helpful to:

- Find and connect with the specific fear
- Describe the fear
- Feel it fully and imagine facing it head on until it has dissipated
- Rationalise it away

It's relatively straightforward, with courage, to do this, and you become quite expert at it.

Then I would imagine me as the child me inside adult me/me as a child facing the same fear head on. This was a lot more frightening but it ensured that I brought the child me along with me during the process, resulting in a new, confident, unified me.

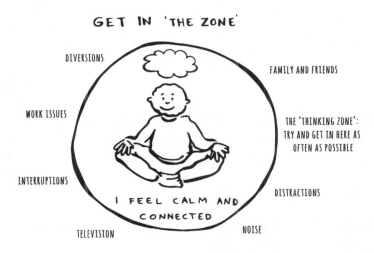

GET IN 'THE ZONE'

DIVERSIONS

FAMILY AND FRIENDS

WORK ISSUES

THE 'THINKING ZONE':
TRY AND GET IN HERE AS
OFTEN AS POSSIBLE

INTERRUPTIONS

DISTRACTIONS

I FEEL CALM AND CONNECTED

TELEVISION

NOISE

After connecting with myself, I then try to collect all my deeply held but repressed fears, feelings, and forgotten parts of me into one mental place.

This is a lot like herding sheep. Some of the sheep are traumatised and scared and try to run away, or to kick out violently. I have to gently coax these sheep into the pen. This takes a bit of time and patience.

D. After Connecting, Unify

THE TORQUEMADA
SELF-PUNISHING
PART OF ME

ANGRY AND
FRUSTRATED
PART OF ME

THE ISOLATED
AND SCARED
CHILD PART OF ME

Connect, understand, be patient with, win trust and coax into 'unified me'.

A UNIFIED ME
WITH NO MORE
INTERNAL FEAR
OR CONFLICT

E. From Searching for Emotional Data to a Tsunami of Data

Compartmentalising My Thoughts

I found it very useful to compartmentalise my thoughts to avoid bringing my emotional issues into other parts of my life.

You will need to compartmentalise your thinking as there will be a constant need to use up any spare thinking capacity to process all the previously repressed and hidden emotional pain and fears.

I found that I had to consciously switch between my different roles in life to give myself the mental space to process the emotional information that I had dug up from my subconscious. It worked a bit like this:

THiNKiNG THERAPY
iN THE SHOWER

BEiNG A PARENT
iN THE BATHROOM

THEN CONSCiOUSLY
PUT YOUR 'WORK HAT' ON

I needed a lot of mental processing power.

Working through all your old emotions and fears requires a huge amount of mental processing power, so you'll often find yourself often feeling mentally fatigued.

F. Overcoming My Fear of My Parents

I was scared of tackling the real threats in my mind.

Tracking my fear of my parents was very scary, yet they were the two key play-makers in the opposing team who would always deliver the key 'killer' ball that would lead to our defeat. As a holding midfield player I simply had to tackle and confront them, as it was the only logical option.

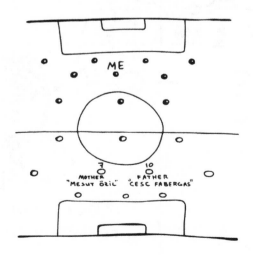

To try and overcome this...

I often used to imagine myself visiting my toddler self and confronting and nurturing him, and warning him about the difficulties ahead, while telling him that I would always be there for him.

I also imagined my father putting his hands on my shoulders in public, showing everybody how proud and supportive he is of me.

I also imagined my mother doing something similar, reminding me of how much she values and loves me.

To help me overcome all the anger, frustration and sense of humiliation I repressed as a child, I imagined the following:

To overcome my theatre analogy mentioned earlier, I would imagine myself as a boy singing angry and loud Metallica and Anthrax heavy metal songs, supported by my childhood best friends, before and in defiance of the audience of extended family members.

Realising the Problem is Not in my Make-Up or Genes

I was glad to realise that depression, shame, low self-esteem etc are much more to do with one's 'nurture' rather than one's 'nature'.

"I'm not genetically deficient." Hurray, a big relief...

The Importance of Learning Self-Compassion

Self-compassion 'is not the same as being easy on ourselves. It's a way of nurturing ourselves so that we can reach our full potential' (Dr Kristin Neff, Associate Professor of Human Development at the University of Texas at Austin). It's a very important trait to learn. More information is available atself-compassion.org/).

Treat yourself like a best friend.

Learn self-compassion.

Learn to speak to yourself, and treat yourself like you would your best friend, if he/she were in trouble.

I found this quite difficult, and even a bit scary to do at first, perhaps stemming from childhood experiences where I looked for affection but didn't receive it.

Realising It Was not My Fault

I found that ridding myself of this deep sense of toxic shame was much more difficult than I had ever thought. I found it useful to complete a Challenging Questions Worksheet used in a form of psychotherapy called Cognitive Behavioural Therapy, aimed at changing unhelpful thinking and behaviour.

Designed to help you overcome deep-rooted 'stuck points' that create strong negative feelings (used in 'cognitive processing therapy').

G. Deconstructing False and Distorted Perceptions

I put my father on a huge pedestal when young, imagining he was this perfectly confident person who had no doubts or weaknesses. I had to gradually deconstruct this image of him in my mind to build a realistic one.

This took an awfully long time and a lot of mental effort to resize my image of him so that I eventually saw him on an equal footing with me.

I also had to deconstruct my mental images of all my pedestal friends, which also took time and effort, but this reframing was very important for me. As with my father, this took a bit of courage as I had to imagine asserting myself over people I had originally believed were much more valuable and impressive than myself.

H. Cutting the Shame Knots that Bind You

This is like speaking Mongolian to my parents. They have no idea they tied me up in knots in the first place. (As I hadn't when it was happening.)

"YOU ARE SUCH A BURDEN"
= 1 KNOT OF SHAME x 1,000
= THOUSAND KNOTS OF SHAME

TOXIC SHAME
SELF-REINFORCING
NEGATIVE THOUGHTS
↓

I HAD TO FREE MYSELF USING THERAPY AND TALKING ABOUT MY FEELINGS FIND MY VOICE AND SENSE OF LEGITIMACY

Imagining or Role Playing Confronting My Parents and Asserting Myself

First imagine me as an adult confronting and asserting myself towards my mother. This shaming of a child is emotional torture with lifelong damaging effects.

IF YOU ARE ANNOYED, THEN TELL ME WHY, YOU STUPID WOMAN, OR TREAT ME WITH RESPECT.

And then, more difficultly, as a small boy (imagining this requires a lot more courage but is very rewarding).

And the same for my father, first an an adult, then...

as a child...

This silent treatment from a father is emotional torture with lifelong damaging results.

Imagining doing it as an adult is relatively easy, but then I found I had to imagine myself as a small boy again, confronting them when I was younger, all those years ago, as a scared child. This was a lot more difficult but also very rewarding and liberating.

Such behaviour from both parents towards a child leads to a sense of being continually judged and scrutinised for apparent wrongdoings with no explanation whatsoever of what these could be. This tortured existence is harrowingly and beautifully captured in Franz Kafka's *The Trial*.

Now I know why I felt such shame. Now I have found my voice, my sense of personal authority and legitimacy. Now I see my closest friends as supportive.

Shame Driven

Overcoming My Toxic, Ultra-Paranoid Thoughts

I feel so ashamed that I could not stop my mother abusing me emotionally. It was such a humiliating experience because it went on for so long as it made me feel so ashamed and emasculated.

ME

"Please tell me you understand?"

REST OF THE WORLD

"Of course we do. You were just a defenceless child who was never allowed to develop any defence mechanisms."

"That makes me feel so much better, thank you! Now I no longer feeling like a weak and pathetic victim who couldn't defend himself."

My Bad Apple Core of Belief

The core of my problem was the false belief that I was not good enough for my parents at a fundamental level. This stayed with me until I uncovered it during therapy. It gnawed away at me and at my core sense of worth all my life until now.

How This Poisoned Apple Core Affected Me

As a child I believed that everybody else knew this 'fact' and wanted to humiliate me accordingly.

Later on in life my parents unambiguously and clearly rid me of this childish and totally false 'core belief' of mine.

This realisation allowed me to imagine myself going to these 'friends' once and for all proving that what (I feared) they were saying was categorically false, allowing me to finally find peace of mind.

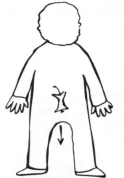

This core, false belief was like a poisonous bad apple sitting in my stomach all my life, unsettling me always. This belief cause me to permanently question my self-worth and made me feel very ashamed of myself for being plainly inadequate. This led me to put huge psychological pressure on myself to always prove myself to everyone.

I've worked out the secret release code! After a lot of soul-searching and help from others, I now know I am worthy of being loved! Click, the lock opens and I'm finally free.

SHAME
LOCK

Real Emancipation from the Effects of My Childhood Experiences Took Years of Effort

This is because changing learned behaviour is much more difficult and demanding than learning behaviour in the first place.

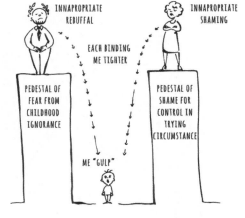

I also now see my parents in a much more realistic light, as real humans, also with their own difficult childhood experiences and associated fears. They grew up in a very different culture when such things weren't spoken about, so I do not blame them at all; they were just trying to do their best, after all.

I. Overcoming Religious Indoctrination

My Experience With Religious Indoctrination

It was vital for me to question and challenge what I was taught. This process, which turned out to be a lengthy and intensive one, really helped me liberate myself from what I now regard as dangerously misleading and belittling beliefs. (Although I understand that others may find their experience of religion a positive one, I would still state that it is all wishful thinking, but that is a debate for another occasion.)

I had to find the courage to question the validity and truth of Christianity and of these 'supreme beings' who could apparently save or destroy me for eternity.

I found this very daunting to say the least.

GOD

THE FATHER

JESUS

THE SON

THE HOLY GHOST

MARY

THE MOTHER
OF JESUS

LITTLE ME

THE HUMBLE LAMB

I also had to come to terms with realising there is in fact no afterlife. This was initially very disconcerting and difficult to accept. However, accepting this makes me value and appreciate each day of my life so much more than before. I also don't have to be submissive to any god, which fills me with self-respect.

I read lots of books on the subject and listened to lots of debates.

These two books really swung it for me and I became an atheist, and I felt so free and liberated.

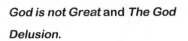

God is not Great and **The God Delusion.**

Overcoming Reliance on Alcohol for Release

10% of issues still scaring/upsetting me. These were the outstanding 'triggers' for my alcohol dependency.

90% of subconscious fears and issues already processed and filed away again with reason and logic giving me 90% peace of mind.

Once I had identified, faced, rationalised and overcome these remaining issues I suddenly felt peace of mind. There were no more ghosts in my basement, no more mental weights dragging me down, no more significant irrational fears, no more deep insecurities that would trigger a flight to alcohol for momentary relief.

Tackling Shame So Future Generations Don't Have To

Shame is passed down the family tree, from one generation to the next, until someone who inherited it tackles it and overcomes it, thus saving future generations from its life-crushing effects.

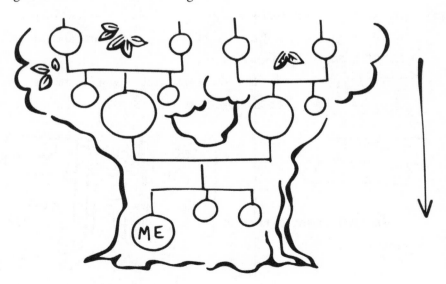

FUTURE
GENERATIONS

ALL THE 'SHAME WATER' COLLECTED
BY PREVIOUS GENERATIONS

EXERTING HUGE PRESSURE

YOU/ME THE VERY
STRONG WALL
OF THE DAM

THE REST OF THE
'SHAME WATER'
CAN BE USED TO
CREATE POSITIVE
CHANGE LIKE
HYDROELECTRIC POWER

A LOT OF THE 'SHAME WATER' DISSIPATES
INTO THE AIR AS IT IS IN REALITY JUST HOT
AIR SOME OF IT SEEPS INTO THE GROUND

WATER REDUCES OVER TIME TO NOTHING
AND THE PRESSURE IS OFF

Brutal Self-Honesty is the Only Way Forward

The vital need to be brutally honest with yourself.

Me looking in the mirror. What am I really scared of? No one else need know, but I need to reveal things to myself that I've been blocking and kidding myself about.

It Can Be a Lonely and Difficult Climb (Just Take One Step at a Time, and You Are Not Alone)

You will most likely feel very misunderstood and frustrated that nobody really knows the hardship you are experiencing. This is because it's very tricky to tell people where you are mentally and emotionally when you don't really know yourself. Alas, you just have to be magnanimous about it.

YOUR ROUTE WITH NO MAP

UNKNOWN DESTINATION

HUGE MOUNTAIN WITH LOTS OF BAD WEATHER NO MAPPED ROUTE

Everybody else's route is easy: easy directions, simple map, nice environment.

Taking and Keeping Brief Notes on Progress

My personal experience is to try and write things down as often as possible. Dreams, fears, issues to discuss at next therapy session, childhood memories, images crossing your mind, topics discussed at therapy and their possible meanings, recent experiences.

Just writing things down often removes the potency of fears and any uncomfortable thoughts.

MY NOTES

Channel Negative Energy Towards Self-Development

Learn how to channel any anger and frustration you feel into positive pursuits like learning new skills (e.g. I learnt a lot about personal finance). This will distract you and raise your self-esteem.

I also really liked reading about cosmology, first in attempt to diminish the sense of toxic shame that I felt by putting myself in this staggeringly vast structure of the universe. I also thought, how can Jesus/God know my thoughts when I'm one of 7 billion people living in a universe with 100,000,000,000,000,000,000,000,000 stars in it?

I also liked reading books on basic philosophy which enabled me to put all my fears and sense of inadequacy into a much broader moral perspective. Certain self-help books were also very useful.

It goes without saying that exercise will really help when going through therapy, and will help maintain much-needed energy levels.

No Regrets

I try to imagine this scenario at the end of my life to motivate myself during the therapy process.

Imaginary bloke who processes us when our time is up. "Sorry mate, no life refunds. You know knew this all along."

"But I haven't done the things I wanted to do yet, like find out who I really am."

If you are going to feel shattered (emotionally, mentally) on occasions, then you may as well learn something from these difficult periods.

There are likely to be periods when you are sleeping badly, or when you are experiencing emotional pain while processing some previous experience and you are just generally shattered. Believe it or not, I found these periods to be some of the most fruitful I had during my recovery process. It is perhaps a cliché, but emotional pain does offer the opportunity for personal growth, and for you to push your emotional boundaries and gain insight into new areas. These periods will include moments of anger and frustration, and I used these emotions to give me the courage and desire to challenge and slay some of my 'sacred cows' (such as questioning my religious indoctrination) that I would not have had the courage to do otherwise.

A 'better' me...

Start of therapy.

**My best hope for who I could become. I surpassed this best hope
some time age and I now have a much more ambitious vision of
who I can be.**

Part 3

Managing the Therapy Process

A. Some Practical Tips

Finding Help

The NHS website offers a comprehensive list of websites and contact phone numbers for seeking help in the UK if you're concerned about yourself or a loved one.

The following websites are useful when looking for someone professional to talk to. In no particular order:

- welldoing.org/
- www.nhs.uk/conditions/stress-anxiety-depression/pages/free-therapy-or-counselling.aspx
- www.itsgoodtotalk.org.uk/therapists
- members.psychotherapy.org.uk/findATherapist

Additional resources include:

- ifucareshare.co.uk
- consolecounselling.co.uk
- samaritans.org

For international support helplines, please visit:

- www.befrienders.org or www.suicide.org/international-suicide-hotlines.html

Taking That Vital First Step and Looking For Help

Be brave and look for help by contacting the organisations out there who are there for you – swallow your pride and just do it! If you don't think people around you will support you, or may even mock you for taking this vital step, then just don't tell them (it most likely shows they are too scared themselves to look for help). Nobody has to know.

'Strength'

Men tend to believe that they have to sort things out by themselves as they should be 'strong' and self-sufficient. This is, of course, nonsense. If you are physically ill, you don't need to be 'strong' and not see a doctor; that's just foolish. If you are having emotional difficulties, then seeking help, such as by seeing a specialist, should be seen in the same light, and should be admired. It will also make you much more emotionally resilient in the future. On the subject of 'strength', take a look at the very influential TED Talk on the subject of vulnerability by Brené Brown. For a proper perspective on the issue of 'strength' and how our society acknowledges 'success', try the excellent *The Road to Character* by David Brooks (also available in summary form via the excellent Blinkist app).

Undergoing Therapy

Try not to take things too seriously on your way to the appointment; humour gives a good perspective on things. Be prepared to face some possible unexpected truths, especially in the first few sessions (e.g. I always thought I had a healthy relationship with my mother, but it quickly became apparent that this wasn't the case, which knocked me back a bit). It's very important to find a therapist you feel comfortable with and you click with. If you don't find the first few sessions useful, then use any extra energy you have to find a different one. Once you find a therapist you feel comfortable with the process becomes much more rewarding and informative (it took me three attempts to find a therapist with whom I felt comfortable, and the process suddenly became very useful for me). Use the therapist session wisely. The therapist is likely being paid well for his/her time and they will very likely have heard whatever you may tell them many times from a huge number of different people. So have a good whinge – this is your time and you have somebody intent on listening to whatever you have to say about anything (it can be quite liberating at times).

I started to see glimpses of a better, more positive me after a few months. This realisation that my fate was not totally fixed and unchangeable, and that I was not doomed to be anxious all my life, was a revelation. If you stick with it these glimpses will increase in frequency and size as you gradually become the real you. All you have to do is stick with the process for as long as you feel it is benefiting you.

Taking Notes

I personally found it useful to write down my fears, insecurities and issues that were bothering me. Putting them down on paper clarified them, gave me a fresh perspective on them, and made them seem more manageable. I also made brief notes after some therapy sessions, noting down things I had learnt about myself and other revelations so that I wouldn't forget them. I also found it useful sharing carefully selected, generic elements of these personal and confidential notes with my partner so as to keep her in the loop on what issues, at a very general level, I was discussing with my therapist. You will likely feel frustrated that your partner doesn't understand what you are going through, how deep the emotional wounds are, and how much mental effort it takes to heal them etc. I felt this way, which led me to decide to share some of these notes in a very careful manner. However, some experts may warn against sharing any notes you may make, regarding this as a breach of the confidentiality that is central to the therapy process.

Confronting the Person(s) Who Caused the Pain?

The question will no doubt arise in your mind as to whether to confront the person who caused your emotional confusion and pain in childhood.

There will most likely be a lot of pent-up aggression and anger and frustration towards this person that needs to be released. One way of doing this is to confront the person in question. However, going in all guns blazing won't help anyone, especially as the person may not even be fully aware of the role they played in what happened all those years ago (as you may not have been until you did therapy). It can be almost like speaking a foreign language when talking about your complex feelings from many decades ago to somebody who may not be the most emotionally intelligent person around (no criticism intended). There are of course pros and cons to confronting these people. On the one hand it may prove cathartic for you to do so. On the other hand, it may stir up a hornets' nest that negatively affects everyone involved.

A book well worth looking at with specific guidance on whether and how to confront the people in your past who played a key role in your ongoing emotional problems is *Toxic Parents: Overcoming Their Hurtful Legacy and Reclaiming Your Life* by Susan Forward and Craig Buck.

I thought long and hard about confronting my parents. For many years I was frankly far too scared to even consider doing it. In my case, I was confronting parents who had no real idea of the negative impact they had had on me when I was growing up. In addition, they are getting rather old, and as previously mentioned, in essence they are very good, kind people whose hearts were always in the right place. In the end, I thought if I could re-channel this childhood anger and insecurity into something positive for me then that would be better for all concerned (although getting to this position took an awful lot of therapy, patience, courage and self-reflection). This gave me a sense of renewed self-respect for having managed my rather primeval emotions, which in turn led to less of a desire to confront my parents. In short, I had risen above the basic urge for retribution and that made me feel a whole lot better, and it also gave me a personal energy boost, as hoped for. By rising above it, I was able to kill two birds with one stone, i.e. overcome my sense of humiliation through renewed self-respect and prevent what might have proved to be a family trauma (involving both parents, my siblings, my wife and our children).

B. Conclusion

It's a pretty simple process, really (with the added ingredients of magnanimity and courage).

In essence, then, finding your way out of despair can be a straightforward process. Seek professional help, come to terms with your past and formative experiences, and move on with magnanimity and renewed self-knowledge, self-respect and new-found wisdom. However, achieving this needs effort, commitment, discipline and no little courage, but the rewards are little short of life-changing.

Good luck!

Annex

Useful Quotes

In one and the same fire, clay grows hard and wax melts.
Francis Bacon

You drown not by falling into a river, but by staying submerged in it.
Paulo Coelho

Your value doesn't decrease based on someone's inability to see your worth.
Anonymous

Stand up and walk out of your history.
Dr Phil McGraw

Some days there won't be a song in your heart. Sing anyway.
Emory Austin

The first step is for man to cease to be the slave of man. The second is to cease to be the slave of the monsters of his own creation, the ghosts and phantoms of the air.
Robert S. Ingersoll

The only person you are destined to become is the person you want to be.
Ralph Waldo Emerson

The secret of getting ahead is getting started.
Mark Twain

We are who we choose to be. Nobody is going to come and save you. You've got to save yourself.
Barry Manilow

Be kind, for everyone you meet is fighting a battle you know nothing about.
Wendy Mass, originally attributed to Ian Maclaren

Our goal is to become a compassionate mess.
Rob Nairn

Stop being a prisoner of your past. Become an architect of your future.
Robin Sharma

Facing it, always facing it, that's the way to get through. Face it.
Joseph Conrad

If you meet it promptly, and without flinching, you will reduce the danger by half. Never run away from anything. Never!
Winston Churchill

Love takes off masks that we know we can't live without and we know we can't live within.
James Baldwin

At first, know yourself.
Anonymous

To be thrown upon one's own resources is to be cast into the very lap of the fortune, for our faculties then undergo a development and display an energy of which they were previously unsusceptible.
Benjamin Franklin

The unexamined life is not worth living.
Socrates

In the midst of winter, I found there was, within me, an invincible summer.
Albert Camus

The best thing you can do with your life is to tackle the shit out of it.
Cheryl Strayed

It's never too late to be who you might have been.
George Eliot

The problem is, you think you have time.
Buddha

He who knows others is learned. He who knows himself is wise.
Laozi (Lao-Tzu)

You can't just hope for happy endings. You have to believe in them. Then do the work, take the risks.
Nora Roberts

Jump, and the net will appear.
Julia Margaret Cameron

We are confined only by the walls we build ourselves.
Andrew Murphy

I have found that if you love life, life will love you back.
Arthur Rubinstein

The happiness of your life depends upon the quality of your thoughts.
Marcus Aurelius

What is good, you ask? To be brave is good.
Friedrich Nietzsche

The doors will be opened to those who are bold enough to knock.
Tony Gaskins

Shame is a soul-eating emotion.
Carl Jung

If your ship doesn't come in, swim out to it.
Jonathan Winters

Sin lies only in hurting others unnecessarily; all other 'sins' are invented nonsense.
Robert A. Heinlein

Never despair. But if you do. Work on in despair.
Edmund Burke

Stop fighting yourself and start fighting for yourself.
The Revolutionary Impact (therevolutionaryimpact.tumblr.com/)

If life is an uphill slog, imagine the view from the top.
Anonymous

Never retreat, never explain, get it done and let them howl.
Benjamin Jowett

When we argue for our limitations, we get to keep them.
Evelyn Waugh

We have a choice: To plough new ground, or let the weeds grow.
US State of Virginia Department of Agriculture brochure, 1959

Opportunity does not knock; it presents itself when you beat down the door.
Kyle Chandler

It is not the critic who counts; not the man who points out how the strong man stumbles, or where the doer of deeds could have done them better. The credit belongs to the man who is actually in the arena, whose face is marred by dust and sweat and blood; who strives valiantly; who errs, who comes short again and again, because there is no effort without error and shortcoming; but who does actually strive to do the deeds; who knows great enthusiasms, the great devotions; who spends himself in a worthy cause; who at the best knows in the end the triumph of high achievement, and who at the worst, if he fails, at least fails while daring greatly, so that his place shall never be with those cold and timid souls who neither know victory nor defeat.
Theodore Roosevelt

To transform the world, we must begin with ourselves; and what is important in beginning with ourselves is the intention. The intention must be to understand ourselves, and not to leave it to others to transform themselves. This is our responsibility, yours and mine; because, however small may be the world we live in, if we can bring about a radically different point of view in our daily existence, then perhaps we shall affect the world at large.

J. Krishnamurti

You get older and you learn there is one sentence, just four words long, and if you can say it to yourself it offers more comfort than almost any other. It goes like this: At least I tried.

Ann Brashares

A man has many skins in himself, covering the depths of his heart. Man knows so many things; he does not know himself. Why, thirty or forty skins or hides, just like an ox's or a bear's, so thick and hard, cover the soul. Go into your own ground and learn to know yourself there.

Meister Eckhart

Trust thyself; every heart vibrates to that iron string.

Ralph Waldo Emerson

Any life, no matter how long and complex it may be, is made up of a single moment in which a man finds out, once and for all, who he is.

Jorge Luis Borges

Almost any difficulty will move in the face of honesty. When I am honest I never feel stupid. And when I am honest I am automatically humble.

Hugh Prather

If you find yourself in the wrong story, leave.

Mo Willems

The most common way people give up their power is by thinking they don't have any.

Alice Walker

You are as amazing as you let yourself be. Let me repeat that. You are as amazing as you let yourself be.

Elizabeth Alraune

We ask ourselves, who am I to be brilliant, gorgeous, talented, fabulous? Actually, who are you not to be? You are a child of God. Your playing small does not serve the world. There is nothing enlightened about shrinking so that other people won't feel insecure around you… And as we let our own light shine, we unconsciously give other people permission to do the same. As we are liberated from our own fear; our presence automatically liberates others.

Marianne Williamson

Further Reading

Brave Enough by Cheryl Strayed

Cognitive Behavioural Therapy For Dummies by Rhena Branch and Rob Willson

Counselling for Toads: A Psychological Adventure by Robert de Board

Daring Greatly: How the Courage to Be Vulnerable Transforms the Way We Live, Love, Parent and Lead by Brené Brown

Feel The Fear and Do It Anyway by Susan Jeffers

Healing the Shame That Binds You by John Bradshaw

Home Coming: Reclaiming and Championing Your Inner Child by John Bradshaw

How to Stay Sane: The School of Life by Philippa Perry

In Defense of Selfishness by Peter Schwartz

Letter to my Father by Franz Kafka

Living with A Black Dog and other books by Matthew Johnstone

Reasons to Stay Alive by Matt Haig

Self Compassion: Stop Beating Yourself Up And Leave Insecurity Behind by Kristin Neff, Ph.D.

Silently Seduced: When Parents Make Their Children Partners by Kenneth M. Adams, Ph.D.

The Art of Thinking Clearly by Rolf Dobelli

The Road to Character by David Brooks

How to Survive Family Life by Oliver James

100 Principles for Seeing Deeply into Yourself and Others by ...MD

...ing Their Hurtful Legacy and Reclaiming Your Life by ...D.

...I Do That? Psychological Defence Mechanisms and the Hidden Ways They Shape Our Lives by Joseph Burgo Ph.D.

If you liked this book I would really appreciate you adding a quick review of it on your favourite sites (it shouldn't take more than a few minutes) and thanks in advance for considering this!

For more information on Luke and his work please go to www.lukepemberton.com

A percentage of sales of this book will be donated to CALM

CPSIA information can be obtained
at www.ICGtesting.com
Printed in the USA
LVHW090040110720
660322LV00003B/318

9 781781 327722